AURORA VON ANGEL

The AI Advantage

Copyright © 2024 by Aurora Von Angel

All rights reserved. No part of this publication may be reproduced, stored or transmitted in any form or by any means, electronic, mechanical, photocopying, recording, scanning, or otherwise without written permission from the publisher. It is illegal to copy this book, post it to a website, or distribute it by any other means without permission.

Aurora Von Angel has no responsibility for the persistence or accuracy of URLs for external or third-party Internet Websites referred to in this publication and does not guarantee that any content on such Websites is, or will remain, accurate or appropriate.

First edition

This book was professionally typeset on Reedsy. Find out more at reedsy.com

Contents

1	Chapter 1	1
2	Chapter 2	4
3	Chapter 3	8
4	Chapter 4	11
5	Chapter 5	14
6	Chapter 6	18
7	Chapter 7	21
8	Chapter 8	25
9	Chapter 9	29
10	Chapter 10	33
11	Conclusion	37

1

Chapter 1

P*ower Up: Demystifying Artificial Intelligence for Business Growth*

Welcome to the age of intelligence augmentation! In this new era, businesses are undergoing a transformative shift, fueled by the power of Artificial Intelligence (AI). But what exactly is AI, and how can it be harnessed to propel your business towards unprecedented growth? This chapter serves as your launchpad into the exciting world of AI, clearing away misconceptions and equipping you with a foundational understanding of its core concepts and terminology.

Mythbusting AI: From Science Fiction to Practical Application

Science fiction has long painted AI as a sentient force, robots taking over the world. However, the AI landscape of today is far more grounded. AI refers to a branch of computer science focused on developing intelligent machines capable of mimicking human cognitive functions like learning and problem-solving.

These machines achieve this through sophisticated algorithms that can analyze vast amounts of data, identify patterns, and make predictions.

The key takeaway? AI isn't about replacing humans, but rather augmenting our capabilities. Imagine having a tireless, data-crunching assistant working alongside you, uncovering hidden insights and automating tedious tasks. That's the true potential of AI for businesses.

The Building Blocks of AI: Unveiling the Technology Behind the Magic

So, how does AI translate complex algorithms into practical applications? Let's delve into some of the fundamental technologies that power AI:

Machine Learning (ML): This is the workhorse of AI, enabling machines to "learn" from data without explicit programming. By analyzing massive datasets, Machine Learning algorithms can identify patterns and relationships, allowing them to make predictions and improve their performance over time.

Deep Learning: A subfield of Machine Learning inspired by the structure of the human brain. Deep learning utilizes artificial neural networks, mimicking the interconnected web of neurons in our brains. These networks process information through multiple layers, allowing them to tackle complex tasks like image recognition and natural language processing.

Big Data: AI thrives on data, the more the merrier. Big data refers to vast, complex datasets that traditional methods struggle to analyze. AI excels at extracting valuable insights from this data, empowering businesses to make data-driven decisions.

CHAPTER 1

A Glossary for the AI Era: Understanding Key Terms

As you navigate the world of AI, encountering new terminology is inevitable. Here's a quick reference guide to equip you with a basic understanding of some key terms:

Algorithm: A set of instructions that a computer follows to perform a specific task.

Artificial Neural Network (ANN): A computer system inspired by the human brain, designed to process information through interconnected nodes.

Machine Learning Model: A software application trained on data to perform a specific task, such as predicting customer churn or identifying fraudulent transactions.

Natural Language Processing (NLP): A branch of AI that enables computers to understand and process human language.

Supervised Learning: A type of Machine Learning where the data is labeled, allowing the algorithm to learn the relationship between inputs and outputs.

Unsupervised Learning: A type of Machine Learning where the data is unlabeled, and the algorithm identifies patterns and relationships on its own.

This is just the beginning of your AI journey. By understanding the core concepts and terminology, you've taken the first step towards unlocking the immense potential of AI for your business.

In the following chapters, we'll delve deeper into the practical applications of AI, exploring how it can transform various aspects of your business and propel you towards achieving sustainable growth.

Chapter 2

Seeing the Unseen: How AI Unlocks Hidden Insights

Imagine a world where your business can see beyond the surface, uncovering hidden patterns and trends buried deep within your data. This is the transformative power of AI in data analysis. In today's data-driven world, businesses generate a constant stream of information – customer transactions, marketing campaigns, social media interactions. But the true value lies in unlocking the insights concealed within this data.

This chapter explores how AI empowers you to "see the unseen" by revolutionizing data analysis and unlocking its true potential for business growth.

The Data Deluge: From Drowning to Discovery

Businesses today are swimming in a sea of data. Every customer interaction, every sale, every click on a website generates valuable information. Yet, the sheer volume and complexity of this data can be overwhelming. Traditional data analysis methods often struggle to keep pace, leaving a treasure trove of insights undiscovered.

Enter AI: The Data Detective with Superhuman Abilities

AI algorithms excel at sifting through vast amounts of data, identifying patterns and relationships that might escape the human eye. Imagine having a tireless data detective working around the clock, uncovering hidden correlations and trends. AI can do just that, offering capabilities that traditional methods simply cannot match:

Unveiling Hidden Patterns: AI's ability to analyze complex data sets allows it to identify subtle patterns and anomalies that human analysts might miss. This can reveal hidden trends in customer behavior, market fluctuations, or even equipment failure.

Connecting the Dots: AI excels at finding connections between seemingly disparate data points. This allows you to create a more holistic view of your business, uncovering unexpected relationships that can inform strategic decision-making.

Predictive Power: By analyzing historical data and identifying patterns, AI can predict future trends with remarkable accuracy. This allows you to anticipate customer demand, optimize marketing campaigns, and proactively address potential problems.

Seeing the Future: Leveraging AI for Predictive Analytics

The ability to predict future trends is a game-changer for businesses. AI-powered predictive analytics allows you to:

Forecast Demand: Accurately predicting customer demand can revolutionize your inventory management and supply chain operations. AI can analyze historical sales data, seasonal trends, and even social media sentiment to anticipate future demand fluctuations.

Target the Right Customers: AI can analyze customer data to identify buying patterns and preferences, allowing you to personalize your marketing campaigns and target the right customers with the right message at the right time.

Identify Potential Risks: Proactive problem-solving is key to business success. AI can analyze data to identify potential risks, such as equipment failure or fraudulent activity, allowing you to take preventive measures and mitigate potential losses.

The Power is in Your Hands: Putting AI-Powered Insights to Work

The insights gleaned from AI data analysis are powerful tools for driving business growth. Here are just a few examples:

Retailers: Use AI to predict customer demand for specific products, optimize inventory management, and personalize in-store and online experiences.

Financial Services: Leverage AI to identify fraudulent transactions, assess creditworthiness, and personalize loan and investment recommendations.

Manufacturing: Utilize AI to predict equipment failure and schedule preventive maintenance, minimizing downtime and ensuring smooth operations.

By embracing AI for data analysis, you'll gain a competitive edge. You'll be able to make data-driven decisions, identify new opportunities, and optimize every aspect of your business for maximum growth. In the next chapter, we'll explore how AI

CHAPTER 2

can further streamline your operations by automating tasks currently performed by your workforce.

Chapter 3

Automation Army: Streamlining Operations with AI

Imagine a workforce where tireless, digital assistants handle repetitive tasks, freeing up your human employees to focus on higher-level functions. This is the reality of AI-powered automation, a revolution transforming businesses by streamlining operations and boosting efficiency.

In this chapter, we'll explore how AI can be your secret weapon for streamlining your operations, allowing you to do more with less and unlock significant growth potential.

The Burden of Busywork: Repetitive Tasks Stifle Productivity

Every business has its share of repetitive, time-consuming tasks. Data entry, generating reports, scheduling appointments – these activities, while essential, drain valuable time and resources from your human workforce. This "busywork" hinders your employees' ability to focus on strategic initiatives and creative problem-solving, hindering overall productivity

CHAPTER 3

and growth.

Enter the AI Workforce: Automating Tasks with Efficiency and Accuracy

AI-powered automation offers a compelling solution. By mimicking human actions with software robots (bots), AI can automate a wide range of repetitive tasks. These bots operate tirelessly, 24/7, with a level of accuracy that surpasses human capabilities. Here's how AI automation benefits your business:

Increased Efficiency: AI bots can tackle repetitive tasks like data entry, form processing, and scheduling at lightning speed, freeing up your employees to focus on more valuable activities.

Reduced Errors: Humans are prone to errors, especially during repetitive tasks. AI bots, on the other hand, consistently follow programmed instructions, minimizing errors and ensuring data accuracy.

Improved Productivity: By automating the mundane, AI empowers your workforce to focus on higher-value tasks that require human judgment, creativity, and strategic thinking. This leads to a significant boost in overall business productivity.

Beyond Efficiency: Unlocking New Possibilities with AI Automation

The benefits of AI automation extend beyond streamlining existing processes. Here are some additional ways AI can revolutionize your operations:

Predictive Maintenance: AI can analyze sensor data from equipment to predict potential failures before they occur. This allows you to schedule preventative maintenance, minimizing downtime and ensuring smooth operations.

Automated Customer Service: AI-powered chatbots can provide 24/7 customer support, answering simple questions and resolving basic issues, freeing up human agents for more complex inquiries.

Automated Fraud Detection: AI can analyze transactions in real-time to identify suspicious activity and prevent fraudulent transactions, protecting your business from financial losses.

Building Your AI Automation Army: A Practical Approach

Getting started with AI automation doesn't require a complete overhaul of your operations. Here's a practical approach to building your AI automation army:

Identify Repetitive Tasks: Analyze your current processes and identify tasks that are repetitive, time-consuming, and rule-based. These are the prime candidates for automation.

Invest in the Right Tools: Various AI-powered automation tools are available, ranging from basic bots to sophisticated machine learning platforms. Choose a solution that best fits your needs and budget.

Start Small & Scale Up: Begin by automating a few non-critical tasks to gain experience and measure the benefits. As you become comfortable with AI automation, you can gradually scale up to encompass more complex tasks.

By leveraging AI automation strategically, you can streamline your operations, boost efficiency, and free up your human workforce to focus on driving innovation and growth. The next chapter delves into the power of AI for customer experience, exploring how you can personalize your customer interactions and build stronger relationships.

4

Chapter 4

The Customer Whisperer: Using AI to Personalize the Experience

In today's competitive landscape, customer experience is the ultimate battleground. Businesses that can personalize interactions, anticipate needs, and build genuine relationships win customer loyalty and drive sustainable growth. Enter AI, the ultimate customer whisperer, empowering you to understand your customers on a deeper level and deliver exceptional experiences at every touchpoint.

The Age of the Discerning Customer: Personalization is No Longer Optional

Customers today have high expectations. They crave personalized interactions, relevant recommendations, and a feeling of being understood. Generic marketing campaigns and one-size-fits-all customer service are no longer enough. Businesses that fail to personalize the customer experience risk losing ground to competitors who prioritize customer needs.

The AI Advantage: Understanding Your Customers Like Never Before

AI empowers you to become a customer whisperer, unlocking a wealth of insights about your customers. By analyzing vast amounts of data, AI can create detailed customer profiles, including:

Purchase History: AI can analyze past purchases to understand customer preferences and buying habits.

Website Behavior: By tracking website interactions, AI can identify browsing patterns and interests.

Social Media Interactions: Analyzing social media conversations allows AI to gauge customer sentiment and brand perception.

With this rich customer data in hand, AI can personalize the customer experience in several ways:

Personalized Recommendations: AI can recommend products or services tailored to individual customer needs and preferences. Imagine an online store that suggests items a customer might like based on their past purchases and browsing history.

Targeted Marketing: AI can personalize marketing campaigns to resonate with specific customer segments. This ensures your marketing messages are relevant and do not come across as generic.

Proactive Customer Service: AI-powered chatbots can provide 24/7 customer support, offering personalized solutions and anticipating customer needs before they arise.

Beyond Personalization: Building Authentic Relationships

with AI

AI offers a boost to customer experience, not a complete fix. However, it can be instrumental in fostering deeper customer relationships. Here's how:

Human + Machine Collaboration: AI excels at handling routine tasks, freeing up human customer service representatives to focus on building rapport and addressing complex issues.

Sentiment Analysis: AI can analyze customer interactions to identify frustration or dissatisfaction, allowing you to proactively address concerns and improve customer satisfaction.

Building Customer Loyalty: By providing exceptional personalized experiences, AI can help build stronger customer loyalty and encourage repeat business.

The Future of Customer Experience: AI as a Partner, Not a Replacement

AI is revolutionizing customer experience, but it's not here to replace human interaction. The future lies in a collaborative approach, where AI handles the data-driven tasks and human expertise focuses on building genuine connections. With the help of AI, we can now understand our customers on a whole new level, therefore you can personalize the customer journey, build stronger relationships, and unlock significant growth potential.

In the next chapter, we'll explore how AI can empower you to make smarter business decisions by leveraging data-driven insights for strategic planning.

Chapter 5

Beyond Human Decision-Making: Leveraging AI for Informed Strategy

Decision-making is the lifeblood of any successful business. But in today's complex and data-driven world, relying solely on human intuition can be limiting. Enter AI, a powerful tool that can transcend the limitations of human cognition, empowering you to make data-driven decisions and develop informed strategies for sustainable growth.

The Duality of Decision-Making: Intuition vs. Data

Business leaders have traditionally relied on a combination of experience, instinct, and available data when making decisions. However, human intuition can be biased by past experiences and emotional factors. Additionally, the sheer volume of data available in today's business landscape can be overwhelming, making it difficult to identify the most relevant insights for informed decision-making.

CHAPTER 5

AI: The Data Decoder and Strategy Augmenter

AI offers a compelling solution to the challenges of data-driven decision-making. Here's how AI goes beyond human capabilities:

Unveiling Hidden Patterns: AI excels at analyzing vast datasets to identify subtle patterns and correlations that human decision-makers might miss. This allows you to uncover hidden insights that can inform strategic planning.

Simulating Scenarios: AI can create complex simulations to predict the potential outcomes of different strategic decisions. This allows you to weigh risks and opportunities before making a final choice.

Eliminating Bias: AI algorithms are data-driven and objective, making them less susceptible to biases that can influence human decision-making. This allows for a more impartial and data-centric approach to strategy development.

Beyond Insights: AI-Powered Tools for Strategic Advantage

AI offers a suite of tools that empower you to leverage data for informed strategy:

Predictive Analytics: AI can analyze historical data and market trends to predict future outcomes. This allows you to make informed decisions about product development, marketing strategies, and resource allocation.

Risk Management: AI can identify potential risks associated with strategic decisions, allowing you to develop mitigation strategies and minimize potential losses.

Dynamic Decision-Making: In a rapidly changing business environment, AI can provide real-time insights and recommendations, enabling you to adapt your strategies quickly and effectively.

The Human Touch: AI as a Partner, Not a Replacement

While AI isn't a magic solution for customer experience, it can be a valuable asset in enhancing human judgment with data-driven insights. Here's how:

Human Expertise with AI Insights: Leaders still possess valuable experience and intuition critical for strategic decision-making. AI provides the data and insights to confirm, refine, or even challenge these judgments for better outcomes.

Collaborative Strategy Development: AI can analyze data and generate various strategic options. However, the final decision and responsibility for strategy execution always lie with human leadership.

Embracing the Future of Strategy: A Data-Driven Approach with AI

By leveraging AI in data-driven decision-making, you can develop and implement more informed strategies, leading to:

Improved Competitive Advantage: AI-powered insights allow you to anticipate market trends, identify opportunities faster, and outmaneuver your competitors.

Enhanced Risk Management: AI helps identify and mitigate potential risks, ensuring your strategies are built on a foundation of stability and growth.

Sustainable Growth: Data-driven strategic decisions informed by AI insights can lead to long-term sustainable growth and success for your business.

CHAPTER 5

In the next chapter, we'll explore how AI can transform your workforce, not by replacing humans, but by upskilling them to collaborate effectively with AI tools and unlock their full potential.

Chapter 6

The Future Workforce: Upskilling Humans Alongside AI

The rise of AI has sparked a wave of concern about automation and job displacement. However, the reality is far more nuanced. AI isn't here to replace the human workforce; it's here to transform it. This chapter explores the future of work in the age of AI, focusing on the importance of upskilling your workforce to thrive alongside intelligent machines.

Beyond Automation: A Collaborative Workforce of Humans and AI

While AI can automate repetitive tasks, the human element remains irreplaceable. Human creativity, critical thinking, and problem-solving skills are more important than ever. The future belongs to a collaborative workforce where humans and AI work together, each leveraging their unique strengths.

CHAPTER 6

AI: The Augmentation Tool, Not the Replacement

Imagine your employees as superheroes, and AI as their powerful new utility belt. AI can handle the mundane, freeing up your human workforce to focus on higher-order tasks such as:

Strategic Thinking: AI can provide data-driven insights to inform strategic decision-making, but humans are ultimately responsible for setting the direction and vision.

Creative Problem-Solving: AI can analyze data and identify patterns, but tackling complex problems and developing creative solutions requires uniquely human ingenuity.

Social and Emotional Intelligence: Building relationships, managing teams, and motivating employees are distinctly human skills that AI cannot replicate.

Upskilling Your Workforce for the AI Era

To thrive in the age of AI, your workforce requires a new skillset. Here's what you can do to upskill your employees:

Focus on Core Skills: Cultivate critical thinking, problem-solving, communication, and collaboration skills across your workforce. These will become increasingly valuable in an AI-driven environment.

Data Literacy: Equip your employees with the ability to understand and interpret data. This will allow them to work effectively with AI tools and extract valuable insights from data analysis.

Embrace Continuous Learning: AI is a rapidly evolving field. Encourage a culture of continuous learning within your organization, allowing employees to stay abreast of the latest AI trends and technologies.

Investing in Your People: The Key to Sustainable Growth

Upskilling your workforce is an investment with a high return. A skilled workforce equipped to collaborate effectively with AI can unlock significant benefits:

Enhanced Productivity: By automating repetitive tasks and empowering employees to focus on their strengths, AI can lead to significant productivity gains.

Increased Innovation: The collaborative human-AI dynamic fosters a culture of innovation, leading to the development of new ideas and solutions.

Improved Employee Satisfaction: Employees who feel empowered with the skills to thrive in the AI era are more likely to be engaged, motivated, and satisfied with their work.

The Future of Work: A Human-Centered Approach

The future of work isn't about humans versus AI; it's about humans and AI working together. By prioritizing upskilling and fostering a culture of collaboration, you can ensure your workforce remains adaptable, innovative, and well-positioned for success in the age of artificial intelligence.

In the next chapter, we'll delve into the practical steps you can take to implement AI within your organization, building a roadmap for harnessing the AI advantage and achieving sustainable business growth.

7

Chapter 7

Building the AI Advantage: A Practical Implementation Roadmap

You've explored the transformative potential of AI, from unlocking hidden insights to augmenting human decision-making. Now it's time to translate theory into action. This chapter serves as your roadmap for integrating AI into your business practices, building the AI advantage and propelling your organization towards sustainable growth.

Before You Begin: Assessing Your AI Readiness

Before diving headfirst into AI implementation, it's crucial to assess your organization's readiness. Here are some key considerations:

Leadership Buy-in: Building the AI advantage requires commitment from the top. Secure leadership buy-in and ensure a clear understanding of the potential benefits and challenges of AI.

Data Infrastructure: AI thrives on data. Evaluate your existing data infrastructure and ensure you have the resources to collect, store, and analyze vast datasets efficiently.

Skills and Expertise: While AI can empower your workforce, a skills gap might exist. Assess your current skillset and consider upskilling initiatives to bridge the gap.

Building Your AI Roadmap: A Step-by-Step Guide

Once you've established your AI readiness, it's time to build your implementation roadmap. Here's a step-by-step approach:

1. *Identify Use Cases*: Don't try to boil the ocean with AI. Begin by identifying specific business challenges or areas where AI can offer the greatest impact. Look for repetitive tasks, data-driven decisions, or areas where insights are hidden within vast datasets.
2. *Prioritize Projects*: Not all AI applications are created equal. Prioritize projects based on their potential impact, complexity, and resource requirements. Start with smaller, less complex projects to gain experience and build momentum.
3. *Assemble Your AI Team*: You don't have to build an AI team from scratch. Leverage the skills you have, identify "AI champions" within your organization, and consider partnering with external AI experts if needed.
4. *Choose the Right Tools*: The AI landscape offers a multitude of tools and platforms. Carefully evaluate your needs and resources when selecting AI tools, ensuring they are compatible with your existing infrastructure and data formats.
5. *Develop a Data Strategy*: Data is the fuel for AI. Develop a

comprehensive data strategy that encompasses data collection, storage, cleaning, and security measures. Ensure your data is high-quality and readily accessible for AI applications.
6. *Implement, Monitor, and Iterate*: AI is not a one-time solution. Continuously monitor and evaluate your AI projects, measuring the impact and identifying areas for improvement. Be prepared to iterate on your approach as you learn and refine your AI strategy.

Beyond Implementation: Building a Culture of AI

Successful AI implementation goes beyond technology. Here's what you need to consider for a smooth transition:

Change Management: Embrace a culture of continuous learning and adaptation. Help your workforce understand that AI is here to augment their capabilities, not replace them.

Transparency and Ethics: Ensure transparency in how AI is used within your organization. Develop clear ethical guidelines for AI implementation, focusing on data privacy, fairness, and accountability.

Communication and Collaboration: Foster open communication and collaboration between business leaders, data scientists, and the workforce. This will ensure your AI initiatives are aligned with business goals and user needs.

The Road to Success: Unlocking Sustainable Growth with AI

Building the AI advantage is a journey, not a destination. By following this roadmap and prioritizing a thoughtful, human-centered approach, you can leverage AI to:

Optimize Operations: Streamline processes, automate tasks, and gain insights that can improve efficiency and productivity.

Enhance Customer Experience: Personalize interactions, predict customer needs, and deliver exceptional service across all touchpoints.

Drive Innovation: Leverage AI for data-driven decision-making, unlock hidden opportunities, and develop new products and services.

The potential for AI-powered growth is limitless. By strategically integrating AI into your business practices, you can unlock a competitive edge, achieve sustainable success, and future-proof your organization for the exciting era of artificial intelligence.

The next chapter will explore the potential risks and challenges associated with AI, and how to develop a robust risk management strategy.

8

Chapter 8

Avoiding the AI Pitfalls: Ethical Considerations and Risk Management

The transformative potential of AI is undeniable. However, as with any powerful technology, AI comes with its own set of ethical considerations and potential risks. This chapter explores these challenges and equips you with strategies for responsible AI implementation and robust risk management.

The Ethical Landscape of AI: Navigating a New Frontier

AI development and deployment raise a host of ethical concerns. Here are some key areas to consider:

Bias and Fairness: AI algorithms are trained on data sets, and these data sets can reflect societal biases. This can lead to discriminatory outcomes in areas like hiring, loan approvals, or even criminal justice.

Privacy and Security: AI relies on vast amounts of data, raising concerns about data privacy and security. Measures must be taken to ensure data is collected ethically, used responsibly, and protected from unauthorized access.

Transparency and Explainability: Many AI algorithms are complex "black boxes," making it difficult to understand how they arrive at decisions. This lack of transparency can raise concerns about accountability and fairness.

Job Displacement: Automation through AI can lead to job losses in certain sectors. Strategies are necessary to mitigate the impact on displaced workers and ensure a smooth transition to a more AI-driven workforce.

Mitigating Risks and Building Trust: A Responsible Approach to AI

By proactively addressing ethical concerns, you can build trust and ensure responsible AI implementation:

Data Governance: Implement robust data governance practices to ensure data privacy, security, and fairness throughout the AI lifecycle.

Human oversight: Maintain human oversight over AI decision-making processes, especially in areas with high stakes or ethical implications.

Explainable AI: Seek out and utilize AI solutions that prioritize explainability, allowing you to understand how AI arrives at its conclusions.

Impact Assessments: Conduct thorough impact assessments before deploying AI, considering potential biases and unintended consequences.

Collaboration with Stakeholders: Engage with stakeholders, including employees, customers, and the public, in conversations about AI development and implementation.

Building a Risk Management Framework for AI

A comprehensive risk management framework is essential for mitigating potential risks associated with AI:

Identify Risks: Proactively identify potential risks associated with your AI projects, considering ethical concerns, security vulnerabilities, and potential biases.

Develop Mitigation Strategies: Develop mitigation strategies for each identified risk. This might involve modifying data sets, implementing human oversight mechanisms, or establishing clear ethical guidelines.

Monitoring and Continuous Improvement: Monitor your AI projects for unintended consequences and continuously improve your risk management practices based on evolving best practices and regulations.

The Future of AI: A Shared Responsibility

Building a future where AI benefits all of humanity requires a collective effort. Here's what you can do to contribute:

Advocate for Responsible AI Development: Support organizations and initiatives promoting responsible AI development and implementation.

Embrace Transparency and Explainability: Prioritize AI solutions that prioritize transparency and allow for human oversight and intervention.

Invest in Upskilling Your Workforce: Prepare your workforce for the future of work by investing in upskilling initiatives that foster collaboration between humans and AI.

The Path to Responsible AI Adoption

By acknowledging the potential risks and prioritizing ethical considerations, you can harness the power of AI responsibly. Building a robust risk management framework and investing in a culture of transparency will ensure that AI is a force for good, driving innovation, prosperity, and a brighter future for your organization and society as a whole.

The next chapter of this book will explore the exciting possibilities that lie ahead in the ever-evolving world of AI.

Chapter 9

Scaling Your Success: Measuring and Maximizing the AI Impact

You've implemented AI within your organization, navigated ethical considerations, and established a robust risk management framework. Now it's time to reap the rewards! This chapter delves into measuring the return on investment (ROI) of your AI initiatives and maximizing the impact of AI for sustainable growth.

Beyond Hype: Measuring the Value of AI

AI promises transformative potential, but demonstrating its true value requires a data-driven approach. Here's how to measure the ROI of your AI initiatives:

Define Success Metrics: Before deploying AI, establish clear success metrics aligned with your business goals. This might involve measuring increased efficiency, improved customer satisfaction, or higher revenue generation.

Track Performance: Continuously monitor key performance indicators (KPIs) to track the impact of your AI projects. Analyze data to identify areas for improvement and optimize your AI applications.

Focus on Business Outcomes: Don't get bogged down in technical metrics. The ultimate measure of success is how AI contributes to tangible business outcomes like cost savings, increased revenue, or improved customer retention.

Maximizing Your AI Advantage: A Continuous Optimization Journey

AI is not a "set it and forget it" technology. Here's how to continuously optimize your AI applications and maximize their impact:

Feedback Loops: Establish feedback loops to gather user input and identify areas for improvement. This allows you to refine your AI models and ensure they continue to meet evolving business needs.

Iterative Improvement: Embrace an iterative approach to AI. Use data and feedback to continuously update and improve your AI models, ensuring they remain effective over time.

Scaling Up for Success: As you demonstrate the value of AI, build a case for scaling up your initiatives. This might involve expanding AI applications to new departments or business processes.

Beyond ROI: The Transformative Potential of AI

While ROI is important, AI's value extends beyond financial metrics. Here's how AI can bring about a more transformative impact:

Empowering Your Workforce: AI can free up your employees from tedious tasks, allowing them to focus on higher-order functions that require creativity and human judgment.

Innovation and Opportunity: AI can unlock new opportunities and fuel innovation by generating data-driven insights and uncovering hidden patterns that might not be readily apparent to humans.

Building a Culture of Data-Driven Decision-Making: By leveraging AI for data analysis, you can foster a culture of data-driven decision-making across your organization, leading to more informed strategies and improved outcomes.

The Future of AI: A Journey of Continuous Learning

The world of AI is constantly evolving. Here's how to stay ahead of the curve:

Embrace Continuous Learning: Encourage a culture of continuous learning within your organization, ensuring your workforce possesses the skills to leverage AI effectively.

Stay Informed: Follow industry trends, participate in professional development opportunities, and stay abreast of the latest advancements in AI technology.

Collaborate with Experts: Consider partnering with external AI experts who can provide valuable guidance and insights as your AI journey progresses.

The Power is in Your Hands: Building a Sustainable AI Advantage

By following the strategies outlined in this chapter, you can unlock the full potential of AI and scale your success to achieve sustainable growth. Remember, AI is a powerful tool, but it's your vision, leadership, and commitment to responsible implementation that will ultimately determine the impact of AI on your organization.

10

Chapter 10

Congratulations! You've embarked on your AI journey, implemented AI solutions, and begun reaping the rewards. But the world of AI is ever-evolving. This final chapter explores the exciting trends shaping the AI horizon and equips you with strategies to stay ahead of the curve and ensure a long-term AI advantage.

A Glimpse into the Future: Emerging Trends in AI

The field of AI is constantly pushing boundaries. Here are some key trends to watch:

Explainable AI (XAI): The demand for transparency and explainability in AI decision-making will continue to grow. XAI solutions will become more sophisticated, allowing users to understand how AI arrives at its conclusions.

Generative AI: This powerful technology can create entirely new content, from realistic images and music to innovative product designs. Generative AI has the potential to revolutionize various industries.

AI for Social Good: AI is increasingly used to tackle global challenges like climate change, poverty, and disease. Expect to see even more innovative applications of AI for social good in the coming years.

The Rise of Edge AI: Processing data at the source, rather than relying on centralized servers, will become increasingly common. This will enable faster decision-making and improve efficiency in various applications.

Human-AI Collaboration: The future belongs to a collaborative workforce where humans and AI work together, leveraging their unique strengths to achieve optimal results.

Staying Ahead of the Curve: A Proactive Approach to AI

The key to success in the dynamic AI landscape lies in continuous learning and proactive adaptation. Here's how you can ensure your organization remains ahead of the curve:

Invest in Research and Development: Dedicate resources to stay informed about emerging AI trends and technologies. Consider partnering with research institutions or universities to gain access to cutting-edge advancements. Major facilities like these constantly publish groundbreaking research. Be sure to look for reputable sources.

Attend conferences and workshops: Industry conferences and workshops offer a chance to hear directly from leading researchers and practitioners. Look for events organized by official groups such as the Association for the Advancement of Artificial Intelligence (AAAI) or the International Joint Conference on Artificial Intelligence (IJCAI).

Keep up with the latest tech blogs and news websites: Many websites offer insightful commentary and analysis on the latest

AI advancements. Look for publications by tech giants.

Engage with the community: Join online communities dedicated to AI discussion. Platforms like Reddit's r/MachineLearning or online forums hosted by major AI companies offer a chance to connect with enthusiasts and experts.

Open-source projects: Contribute to open-source AI projects. This allows you to learn from experienced developers and get hands-on experience with cutting-edge tools and techniques.

Competitions and challenges: Participating in AI competitions allows you to test your skills against others and gain exposure to new approaches.

Experiment and play: Many companies offer online platforms where you can experiment with pre-trained AI models and tools. This is a great way to get your feet wet and explore new possibilities.

Develop your own projects: Try working on your own personal AI project. This allows you to delve deeper into specific areas of interest and gain practical experience.

Remember, the field of AI is constantly evolving. By staying curious, engaged, and willing to experiment, you can stay on top of the latest advancements.

Foster a Culture of Innovation: Encourage a culture of innovation within your organization, where employees feel empowered to experiment with new AI applications and explore creative solutions.

Develop a Future-proof AI Strategy: Regularly revisit and update your AI strategy to ensure it aligns with evolving trends and remains future-proof.

Embrace Continuous Learning: Upskilling your workforce in AI literacy and fostering a culture of continuous learning will be crucial for adapting to the ever-changing AI landscape.

The Future of Work: Thriving in an AI-Powered World

The future of work will be shaped by human-AI collaboration. Here are some key considerations:

Focus on Core Human Skills: Cultivate critical thinking, problem-solving, creativity, and communication skills within your workforce. These uniquely human skills will remain invaluable in an AI-driven world.

Reskilling and Upskilling Programs: Invest in reskilling and upskilling programs to equip your workforce with the skills needed to collaborate effectively with AI and thrive in the future of work.

Building an Agile Workforce: Develop an agile workforce that can adapt to new technologies and changing business landscapes. Encourage a growth mindset and a willingness to embrace continuous learning.

The Power of AI: A Force for Good

AI has the potential to revolutionize every aspect of our lives, from the way we work to the way we solve global challenges. Here's how you can contribute to a positive AI future:

Advocate for Responsible AI Development: Support initiatives that promote responsible AI development and implementation, focusing on ethical considerations and human well-being.

Bridge the AI Divide: Work towards ensuring equitable access to AI for all, mitigating the risk of an AI divide that widens the technological gap between different sectors of society.

Embrace the Potential for Positive Change: Be an advocate for the positive potential of AI. Use AI to create a more sustainable, equitable, and prosperous future for all.

11

Conclusion

Final Word: The Future is Bright

A The journey with AI is just beginning. As you navigate the AI landscape, remember this: AI is a powerful tool, but it's your vision, leadership, and commitment to responsible implementation that will ultimately shape the impact of AI on your organization and the world. By embracing AI with a proactive, human-centered approach, you can ensure a bright future where AI empowers humanity to achieve remarkable things.

www.ingramcontent.com/pod-product-compliance
Lightning Source LLC
Chambersburg PA
CBHW040337220526
45473CB00009B/2710